THE LULL AND THE WHIRLWIND

SUBIR KUMAR SEN

INDIA • SINGAPORE • MALAYSIA

ISBN 979-8-89026-013-0

Contents

CR PARK

Long, quite long ago when the
Seventies had just begun
Forward came the populace in this area forsaken
Fields forlorn except spiny bush would
Spring up more often
Plains undulating into plateau and recess unmarked
Summers hot beyond conception
Winters cold, unusual.
In the airy expanse would fly winged insects of hues and shades at
Contrast one with the other
Firm land below witness to the crawl
Someone their flight to smother.
Dreariness accompanying sun at its zenith
Rocks embalmed in the yellow rays beneath
Still night further intensified by invisible crickets
Glow-worms afloat.
Shops came into existence gradually
As did we humans
Barren stretches of land bore firm concrete abodes
Beautified now and then
Earth being dug deep down men perspiring.

The Aravali foothills were in possession of a
Queer obsession
That of unraveling the mysterious deep of
All it had in its keep.
There, then was the wood
Green olive dark
Blackened furthermore at dusk.
In the houses few the advent of night would
Bring electric lights spread wide.
Insects would swarm
Of note being the tubular green praying mantis
Clasping its forelegs which it did have one and another
Straining its neck and forging acquaintance.
Day saw red aerials attracted to flowers
Grasshoppers yellow and green
Swarming in flocks.
With thundering pace on the
Earmarked autumn eve the
Refuge did heave with
Resounding beating of the drums
Rendered into full flowing ease by
Weather-beaten eastern brethren.
Drama, folk theatre
Darkness glorified by motion pictures all had
Their day tall.
Cultural events, ceremonies, food

Lethargic noon and the kites in concentric circles
Mighty Durga's yellow forehead
Face ruddy wed
Lost themselves unto Time.
Migratory birds have flown across the locale times without number.
Jet black roads coming up
Arid noon broken by an automobile red
In a rickshaw's stead.
In eddies that rise within
We swirl, commotion fed.

IT'S ME MUKUL

My name is Mukul
Born five and twenty years ago in
Addition to six months the
Childhood had me awestruck by
Novelties daily encountered.
The wonder went on the wane when
Years added on free and
Made a youth of me.
Many a dream did I contemplate of which
Materialized a few
The rest to me due.
The revolution within oft did take place
On occasions slowed down, too, its pace.
The evening the clock struck half past five
Had a face-off with the sun and fields with paddy replete.
Was it heaven?
The aircraft in ruins on the desolate field
Noon encircling I remember having seen.
On entering a dwelling
I partook of nectar.
Is not it kaleidoscopic!
I think a restive spirit seizes hold of you on

Attaining an age
When the blood gushes in fury
Akin to a sea in turmoil.
Much later everything is placid
Like a temple in wilderness.
For instance, me
Striving to foresee the future, in a stupor
Is there any need for it?
By the way, were you present the day the
Early morning sky was overcast and
Piercing winds blew down the alley!
What a terror-stricken call the sky let out at the
City below!
Can you recall the lilting raindrops melodious
Dropping amidst the remote vernal lake?
Strange was the meditative splendor.
On retrospection the
Spoken word suffices not.
Take, for instance, lilac – a color.
Can anyone describe lilac?
Or inhibition?
If you happen to see galactic lights
Stellar, bright the night above and
Myself deprived of the same
Then I am in the dark.
The multi-hued rainbow is brilliant though.

NATURE

Seated upon a tawny boulder, Aravali around an
Azure sky spread above while
Autumnal breeze the crevices touch
Restive peafowl dazzles in the sunlight
Akin to an iridescent gem
Distant green speaks of a landscape commendable
Fixture broken only by the camel bobbing up and down
Approaching like a sea wave with gentle breeze for accompaniment
Withered trees sun-burnt
Butterflies in flight flutter around
Village backyard morose and dull
Boasts of no man
Stone Age having encompassed all in its vice like grip
Regal strictures along to sweep.
Descent down the hill brings a locale steeped in rusticity
Sunrise, the lunar wax and the wane had
Exposure enough to the inhabitants
Rural temple topped with spire
Thronged by the devotees

Dawn advancing cow dung cakes stick to the clay walls the
Niches of which knick knack contain
Highland bird hovers above a
Buffalo dark chews cud beneath a tree its
Mouth with froth whitened
Ill-fitted here the
Land being that of camels and peafowl the
Hill spoken of earlier
Stands in its former place and when
Darkness swooped down at dusk that day it
Put on the garb of an ancient civilization
And its mysterious innovation
Silver ornaments tinkling at night
Jackal howling at the far end.
A bonfire lights up beneath the acacia
When humanity is deep asleep
Dark night
With no sound pervading with might
Two oscillating eyes peep out from the hole have
Me scurrying for cover
Afflicted with fright.

DEATH

So you met the deadly messenger yesterday it
Must be clear there is no time left
He asked you to be prepared by tomorrow.
With so many bygone days
Today would be one more addition
Why did your Virtue and Vice remain unknown?
You think God is what matters
You mean the unseen force
He must be knowing all this.
Where has the elevated spirit gone?
You are lonely within as
You stand with immense difficulty and with
One stroke of a finger would
Drop down alive.
Is then there a way out after death?
You had dreamt a lot
Amidst green fields.
You want to relate, to go on relating
Like the sea waves which burst upon the shores
Every day, each hour.
Are these only emotional exercises?

On that night, too, lighting up the blue lamp behind the green blinds
You had your face covered.
In nineteen eighty seven, Shankharitola Street
Who was the one after walking a small distance
Merged into the Renaissance statuette?
The person you spoke of in your first outcry
Is the one you would like to meet?
If you meet thereafter
Would you sit dazed
With a shudder down your spine?
The massive banyan rural
Afforded a view of the venomous snake.
You tasted pancakes nearby and faces innocent.
Stop, he is approaching.
You can feel the tremor.
Can't you see the dark sky black overcast
All set to commence the strangle?

THE CLOCK AND THE LIZARD

I knew this would happen.

Did not I ask you to escape the city lights to vast open unbound?

But you did not pay heed.

Do you understand now why I said so?

Now everything is lifeless here

Bricks, concrete, high walls.

At times a worn cat would cross the lane, just like you.

What do you say, I should go away?

Even if I go would you feel at ease with yourself?

I knew you will lock the door and gaze at the sky through the ventilator in a

Pensive mood.

You are unable to think.

Where has your philosophy fled?

It has gulped you down like the

Pillar corroded in the lane adjacent.

You want to cry but you are unable to.

Can anything be more painful?

Do not infer that I am unperturbed at the

Plight that is yours but
I cannot bear the sight of you in turmoil.
No, no, do not go for annihilation.
Are you mad?
When a lifeless body would swing
In the urban air.....
No, no, I just cannot think of it.
Well, then, I leave you.
You should be left alone for some time.
Do you remember Beach on Sea, do you remember the sea at noon?
How azure it was!
And have you forgotten the green dragonfly chase?
Do you feel like crying?
Do cry.
You have not wept for ages.
How lovely you used to be!
How restive, like the deer in the woods!
Something befell you later, much afterwards
Reclining on the divan all the while
You would gaze at the clock and the
Lizard, unceasingly.
There were dark circles around your
Eyes, your tired eyes.
Eh! You are weeping.
Good, but still I fear as if

Possibility is only Possibility
Actually, it is too late
If you can forget, do please.

THAT WHICH IS IN ACCOMPANIMENT TO A CHILD

I am but a child seated in the classroom
The smell of bread, butter and sugar all
To me avails throughout the day's length.
I behold elves, gnomes, flowers and beasts alike
Pasted on to the walls, with wonder.
Through the window could be discerned
The shrub in sway.
Tales of demoniac proportion and fairies are related to us
And during fairs
Dolls do abound in our vicinity.
Hardened egg shells, soft cotton and feathery down
Iridescent paper, glue and sundry doth
Take bulbous buttons into their custody
To exchange their individualities
For puppets, elegant and gaudy.
The adjoining house exhibits in unison
A ripened old man and the contents of archaic ways.
Sparrows and pigeons do glide down

When the sun peeps below at the town
To the call of scintillating water
Or else to seek refuge in
Holes which in abundance to them cater.
The mistress, benevolent and kind
Carries me away although for a while.
Magic shows are there to entertain
As is the buoyant dog and its pranks
Following in its train.
The budgerigar in suspended animation
Has its hue in equation with the tiny tots in visitation.
I partake of a crimson candy sweet
With care utmost and discreet
And if a mischance does advent
The orb is picked up
My backbone is bent.
Before rain makes its presence felt
The sky assumes a distinct black.
The earthworm crawls out of its burrow
Water down under.
I stick to the wall with a frown
The icy wall freezes the cheek
Sending forth calcified shudder.
Trickle and splash abound
Distant and around
Of scarce renown.

The blowing wind, deafening roar around
Fears alien cast.
The book abounding in tales
Open lies on the desk
Boasts of a hirsute bear
In a forest, thickets and groves ajar
Carries me away to land afar
Strange and dark
Of draconian rules and measures stark
None dare tread the realm wherein hark
Sabre toothed canines and fiery ark.
A day out kneeling down
Smell of verdant grass.
A stag in brown study
Across the barbed fence
And the massive tree trunks ajar
Archaic and grand spread far.
Ants in a row crawl up the wall
In response to brethren call.
Day drawn out evening abound
Empty, desolate classroom
Ox articulating doom around.
Clock in sway across the wall
Apparitions mobile from void spring tall
With ease consummate and rare
Traverse everywhere.

The puppet, toil and all
Stationary lies in wait for the call
Wields a sword in its hand
As if a magic wand.
The classroom is pale, forlorn
Strongly set in concrete worn.

PREHISTORIC SELVES

I know that it might strike you monotonously
But did you not experience this previously
To wishful thinking transformed resolutions adamant, deadly.
In actuality the future wavers
Turning that which foreseen to quiver
Until to futility transfixed are thy labors.
The itinerant man's desire
To forsake all and tread upon lands of quagmire
Though encounters revolving eyes and the allied ire
Is lofty and high, surpassing the tallest spire.
Furrowed field plural
Set in surroundings rural
Richly yield palm and the accompanying pond
Together with the passing blond
When in unison all
Issue forth a pastoral call
To which poor me enshrouded in pall
Strikes his head against the leaden wall.
Dilemma is written all over
So is the dragonfly in its aerial hover.
Do I lack courage?

Why then does futurity in outrage
Withhold the answer in dark ferrous cage?
The protestors on the move in Dhurumtollah
Seeking answers in the tropical summer, hot and tawny do
Remind me of the status
Which is, and, to be, mine, without hiatus.
Essentially, I am dead
To inanimate objects wed.
Behold the potter creating earthenware
To damnation doomed after arduous care
Shops and the markets wherein they be
Boast of produce on display or under lock and key.
How do I identify myself!
A man, a score and twenty years old
On a fateful day I would
To fragments be torn, being old.
Philosophy, Attachment, Senses
Delirious man's outpouring of grievances
The oft repeated words would be aired with a sigh
The sun, the fields, the sky
And the air in circuitous fashion rising high
Wonder to the brim it does imply.
Better still is wealth
Amassed by means fair and stealth
Behold my dare
Fun and frolic over

I chide a handful of boys to cover
Arrogance in sway likened to a lover
Having acquired regal fancies
I have mistaken life for a field of pansies.
It is sad that men are mortal
Who knows what happens thereafter
Moreover, ought we to know the sequel
Content as we are with feasts and laughter.
Now, the question that out weans is to
Whom I owe my allegiance?
I have decided to answer late
As time enough is there to wait
My name is Adam
Eve, by her proximity to me, the mate.

ME, SHE AND LIKEWISE

Having been mortally clad
In an attire hastening to its doom
To ideas strange access he had
Akin to one experienced by a flower in bloom
Thus the man in question opined
Well worth it was to look within
And the abysmal depths to find
Toppling hurdles rooted firm therein
In the course of the flowing train
Wherefrom did issue forth Sun
Bespangling the dark and horrid lane
In splendor regal which match could none
But for the lunar halo
Encircling an oriental castle
Besides a river shallow scented mellow
Having for company the serpentine rustle
Giving in to the gentle chirrups
As the solar emanation high above
With the rustic earth down below sups
The bewitching eyes transfix his love
Upon she whom youth has in its throes
To the visitations of melancholy subject

In unison fashion raising her brows
Far removed from things petty and abject
When in meadows tawny the two execute vows
Attuned to the wondrous chimes
The cuckoo hawk's gaze and the eagle high
The dual hearts throb, his with her rhymes
So does the bumblebee and the damselfly
In circuitous hover buzzing alike
Past lakes and glades where croaking lie
Country frogs who their prey do strike
When the time be high in natural lap
Wherein rest I, she having narrowed the gap.

WOMAN I KNOW OF

Pen down the known and do not
What you know not.
If you know of women
Striking out amongst men
Who have cast spell
Only to toll your death-knell
Spell out their names.
To utter damnation flung would be their aims.
If you know of a dame
By whose virtue you have none aflame
But on the contrary
Lulled asleep are those weary
Do reveal who they are.
With angels would they be on par.
To virtue and vice in equation subject
He has been through moods tender and abject.
May I recount the tale of a woman horrid
Who dusk befallen bespoke torrid
With demoniac forms visitations made
In a span of hours few bade youth fade.
Fingers gnarled and twisted hurled
Youth thrice away in its stead.

May I recall, too, she who blushed
When my footstep towards her advanced
In nocturnal ecstasy were we clasped
Until the diurnal hour followed one elapsed.
She is the one who exudes feminine grace
Lilting and soft, eager for my embrace.
O woman! Who was it that had you
Girdled in forms benevolent; undue.
To whom should we owe our sustenance
For acquainting us to the countenance
That frets and curses, kisses and drowns
Our sorrows, relieving them of all frowns.

ON THE BRINK OF HOPE

Sitting upon the boulder placed
Along the sidewalk
We talked about our endeavors to
Make artless forms
He related his tale
I recollected mine.
To our right stretched the
Sunflower in growth and
Beyond the fields
Traversed a few trucks on the
Selfsame road.
The raised pathway had a
Locality populated by the not so
Affluent, a distant behind the
Sun was on the wane but
Not so our spirits.
Anticipating the future, we thanked it.

AWAY IN THE COUNTRY

When the child in him to the elder queried
What to him did pleasure mean
The last mentioned had for the reply
Brooks, rivers, daisies and hollyhocks
The mild mildews, the violets subdued
The deafening roar of the boulders loose
Which in heaps did pile up alongside
Nimble-footed frolic
Skipping in dales and vales wherein
The country inn which boasted of
Spicy, nut brown ale brought
In a carriage carted to a horse
Screeching to a halt besides a
Thicket embedding crickets aloud
Did dawn upon the man
The who did sit under the sun, bright aflame.

THE BANYAN TREE

A single seed which accidentally had fallen on the
Earth sprouted forth into a
Herb which by gradual degrees
Grew till it came to be known as a
Shrub which ceaselessly elongated
Itself into a tree which sideways
Spread too traversing circuitous routes in
Directions all making claim to its
Fame throughout the neighbourhood as
One which was huge, massive
Tall and verdant which made some
Green with envious fury springing
Out of abysmal depths wherein
Dwelt hatred in metallic cage
Clanging and banging with ferrous
Rage bent on vanquishing peace and
Things sublime which do gently smile.

HIDE AND SEEK

When monotony decided to cast its spell the
Angel spelt it out in a tender fashion when
Depression crept forward slowly the
Aforesaid soothed me to normalcy.
The battle between good and evil is old indeed.
When Man first appeared on this earth he
Roamed about like a tramp and saw the
Bright day and the dark night.
Memories of bygone summers and winters made Him conscious.
He saw floral creepers, he saw thorny bushes.
He saw the contrasting tiger and deer.
If one saunters across the dew fed grass at dawn a
Gentle touch is applied on.
The dusk has light moon rays, exhilarating.
When an orange flower on a green leaf
Peeps out of a grey city
Fancy rushes out like a fire cracker on wheels.
Births take place, so do deaths and the
Sandwiched years are futile games.
Anger, agony, joy and love
Rent the air and the sky tumultuous after

Birth takes place.
Then all of a sudden one day
Like power snapped away
The body and the soul part ways.
History and Philosophy
Down the ages have
Informed us of facts, figures, schools of thought
Selecting them out with great care.
Today, shorn of clothes if
One makes his way through a forest in a
Feast of red flowers and
Finds a waterfall right across he would be
Overwhelmed with joy.
Once, six days in succession
Illness and depression came in as guests.
We have seen the past, are living in the present.
Those six days the wooden blinds of central Calcutta
Made way for the future.
Future let loose a reign of terror and
Indicated the state of affairs to live up with.
The sweet scented odour which
Permeated the room was made to disappear to exile.
Once half the clouds in the sky made it bright and shady, alternately.
The image of a dark sky through the
Tinted glass of the city bus and the

Contrast it offered to the otherwise blue is
Hard to wipe out.
There is this spot where everyone dumps refuse
Behind the hospital, the virus swarm in numbers.
It is said that the desert is hot
Like the sun's boiling pot.
In its spite, the nor'easter blows over the sylvan country.

THE POEM WRITER

The poet is all set to write a poem
Often walking past away the
Men residing yonder being witness.
He glances at the human forms in the lane
Sipping tea, meanwhile.
The poet is walking again.
Mud splatters the road wet he
Foresees the advancing monsoon.
The poet has behaved thus, earlier, too.
He has walked, he has contemplated.
Some encaged parakeets squawk loud.
In this sweltering heat of June when the
Metalled road softens down
Has the poet ever imagined that
Perspiration would be his lot?
He loves the sky, the stars.
When he went to the forest
Last year, rapt in attention he was.
He sports a long beard not having
Shaved the past four or five months.
The friendly salon is right ahead, accessible.
No, he rubs his chin rather.

To weep is difficult indeed.
The poet weeps, too, at
Night, in a room desolate
Cold rag pressed against the hardened face.

ON COMPOSING A POEM

I know not what to write.
I suppose I had said this on a
Previous occasion, too.
I had said this for a
Likening situation had me in its thrall
Much earlier.
On clear thought, is there anything at all to be said?
Even if I say something
Would it be an invention?
Whom do I describe?
It would be better if the
Identity of all those left out is unknown.
But are they unknown?
If you ask me to speak about myself
I would disclose that
I am engaged in composing a poem.
I am dwelling upon thoughts which can be thought of
Plausible, as well as framed.
In the realm of fancy
Pictures do abound
Kaleidoscopic all.

TO CATCH ONE'S FANCY

Written many decades ago
Presented it to someone a year after
Thought it was not worth it.
Laid gathering dust almost three decades when
I had this urge to make it public
Few years back.
I have been trying to do so for the last three years.
Now came the moment.
On the lookout for someone to publish the poem for
Maximum reach so that
Access is gained to the literary fraternity.
This holds good for any work, I suppose.
No, this is simply an art form, so to say.
I do not want to sound thus but the
Better you perform
More are your chances of making it big
Only if the work is worth it.
You know how human nature is.
Do not try to decipher much
Glide through and enjoy the word play
Just sway to the rhythm

Anyway, she remains to be unraveled to this day.
It is only a poem to be
Read for pleasure
Provided it pleases you.

OF ASTRONOMICAL PROPORTION

The spatial mass downward hurled
By friction lost, shed and rubbed
A glorious blaze trailed behind
Of fire and light sideways and hind
A meteoric rise, nay fall I find
Which match could none however it tried
'Twas visible to apparatus astronomical and kind
Could scarce discern the naked eye n'mind
The majestic delight
The regal flight from celestial height
The leaden lump energized fright
From slumber awoke the wrong and right
To behold the spectacle burning bright
Silver and blue metallic might
Illumined streaked black night.

WAYS AND MEANS SERPENTINE

No sooner did the snake slid unwind
A terrific train trailed behind
Of gravel and dust and bands wide
Of dread and venom personified
Which annihilate it would
Wherever it could
Men and kin true and good
The arduous toil notwithstanding to
Clear the thickets and groves upright
The serpentine terror and fright
Which reigned till day to the dismay
Of all and sundry
In the dale and up close vale
Which the tropics fed again and again
With salt and sweat, moist rain
Thunderous bolt and slant drain
As could thrive the dark reptile
Of deadly fangs in rank and file
A magnanimous form magnified
In the scheme of things ordained lied

Bends and curves deftly hide
Let loose upon with which we vied
Day in and out, summer ignite
Sun scorched up, the ensuing bite.

IS THAT YOU

The woman aged enough to counter the woes
The wicked designs, the evil throes
Stood upright in spite of her plight
And bade the fright take to flight
While she rose above the downward pull
To take to the skies complete and full
To bask in the sun, to float in the cloud
To dance in joy and shout aloud
The spirit exalted and brightly hued
Did gain the more in multitude
The white fluff, the azure up
The yellow rays, the delicious sup
Of fragrant naught, the nimble veer
Heavenly thought sublime and cheer
Courage summed up crystal and clear
High above far and near
Resolute descended after decide
Notwithstanding scoff and deride
Yonder, there and worldwide
Head held high brimming pride
At full moon, at high tide
Still held up personifying pride.

THE DARK CORMORANT

The cormorant dark outstretched perched on
Dead stump o'er raised ground to
Shorn away the wet self and
Come out sleek and dry the
Wings spanned out
Head sideways the
Glossy sheen glistened aloud a
Sight not uncommon in wetlands abound
In lakes and lochs of liquid make and
Dive it would the watery hunt for
Fish and Pisces fresh and sound then
Quite emerge the prey in its throes
Juggled and tossed all
Beaked awhile
Before gulped down and
Further below the dive commenced for
Aquatic prized
Possession held
Twice and thrice, more and often
Morn and noon outstretched lurked
Rose above the risen sky

Feather shrugged off the
Bird's travail a
Weathered tale of
Cormorant black hearty and hale.

ODE TO A MANGO

Ripened fruit long discerned
On paper glossy and upturned
In actuality real and true
Would steer past all through
The touch, the feel magical
The scent profuse theatrical
Rouses forth hunger pang
Quick, fast, a loud bang
Sliced through with a knife
Laughter, friends and some life
Yellow juicy luscious pulp
Ready to devour and down gulp
To savor the bite, the lick inside
The aroma spread round and wide
Drops and splash mellowed lie
Lost alas for flies to vie
Rest consumed by you and I
Oh Mango, you make us die
By flavor unheard, unseen
Fruit oblong yellow and green.

THE BOOK AS WAS

The medieval book hard leather bound
In gradual degrees enlarged abound
Lay quite immersed in the set of drawers
To be read in the study or the towers
For the smell of strong weathered must
Of rightful descent and just
Pages browned out and dust
Of erudite scholars' wet thirst
For knowledge unseen, unknown
Wisdom antique abundant renown
Gathered down the ages sown
To reap the harvest and now own
Cantos and folios penned away
In full flowing ease and sway
Much to the chagrin and dismay
Of critics and dissidents kept at bay
For reasons known and quick to discern
Authors' woes and deep concern
For overcast skies and drowned out sun
Coarse innuendos and coarser pun
Unbecoming of the labor and toil

Arduous hours and pathos loyal
Clung to my bosom, my heart throbs
Life brims joy, death sobs.

EVERY CRAB HAS HIS DAY

The yellow-bellied crab
By no means drab
Swam in the seas
The Bay Indies
Got entangled in the net
Fishing folk cast at the onset
Released on the shore
A sight you would adore
Sold awhile to men 'n women alike
Sell who would further with a hike
To serve as a gastronomical delight
For the rich and connoisseurs' bite
Climbed meanwhile and scaled the side
Of basket hand-woven and wide
At pinnacle reached
And prying eyes breached
Scaled down on the golden sand
The grey and yellow concealed band
Walked sideways the roar dear
Claws quick and sharp lateral clear
The waves grey greyer and blue

The sky above a bluer hue
Made good the escape
The crunchy drape
The brave crustacean
In brinish oblivion
Forever to swim in joyous joy
With a mate for company
In silent cacophony
Endearing and coy.

IN UNISON WE STAND

The windswept day further advanced
Noon past swaying clothes hung
Household surround
In downtown crowd
Through lanes and alleys in garden sound
Flowers and buds sprout scent around
Branches taut and hanging forth creepers abound
Beneath canopy round
Dark and green
Yet unseen
The flowing attire
Impending quagmire
Dust and pollen spread embed
In hair dishevelled
Black and brown face pretty concealed
To conversation revealed
Lips and cheeks and motion meek by
Wondrous drizzle thus cleansed
The throbbing heart, the reddened ear
The gush, the rush, the latent fear

Of distant revelation, though unfounded
Brushed aside by trembling faces rounded
Rhapsody clear.

A FLASH OF SCARE

I woke alarmed to thunder loud
Blue lightning and grey cloud
Cold environ flashing shroud
The neighborhood shone intermittent proud
The wire snapped and broke in two
I ran amok much ado
Many more in the queue
It was a sight fit to view
Impending peril to undo
Imminent danger risky, too
Water droplets vertical fell
Few fleeting drops away as well
In a while the volume did swell
In no time did the sky pour hell
The distant oak all covered in maze
The elm as well difficult to gaze
No way out but to get daze
'Twas indeed a torrid phase
To endure the moment
Stretched full bent
No way left out to vent

The fear, the tremble, the current
Till passed the hour noon and after
Made way to smile peals of laughter
I lay down gently to coos and chirrup
One pancake and some syrup.

THE BIOSCOPE MAN

The Bioscope carrier would frequent its way
Often past obstacles
Into our lane
Making us rush out to
Get a feel of still bright images
Fleeting past to the accompaniment of
Music loud and sound
Not that we could get direct access but
Wait we would
Our turn awaited the
World of melody and colors
Encased in the wooden box
Wheeled around by
Gentle turns and shoves in the
Neighborhood turned amicable by
Entertainment just, fragile a
Penny, a cent, a paisa would suffice to
Gain access to frolic and fun which
Approached in the afternoon and the
Day after and the days subsequent
In the sixties

Not to be seen thereafter as
Vanish it did with the
Evolution of
Gadgets more refined.
On a grim day
You still encounter the Bioscope man
Going through it all
Albeit in a dream into
Oblivion faded
Distant, unseen.

THE LOST KALEIDOSCOPE

I had this crude kaleidoscope of mine
Elongated oblong to carry its role on a
Dull drab day would
Reflect colors of all shades and hues on the
Face as well lightened up by
Maneuvers clockwise and otherwise in the
Attic secluded, lonely as
None would frequent up
Besides me, myself and I
Accompanied by the toy
Thus equipped with a multitude of
Shards, shattered, broken on
Purpose to project the
Earth wrought with joyous joy and
Fulfillment to the brim
Overflowing with desires and intent
Noble, pristine.
I discovered it the other day
Underneath refuse
Accumulated over decades.
I could do no more than wear a smile.
It whistled back.

AT THE END OF THE DAY IT MATTERS

I spotted a grey strand of hair the
Other day on the
Mirrored surface
Amidst the otherwise black locks.
The moustache, too, followed suit.
I made my way to the balustrade
Got myself comfortable in the settee
Sipped a hot cup of tea
Fragrant black
Ventured out and got drenched in the
Morning dew
Ambled up and down the garden.
The risen sun further rose
Flowers blossomed
Trees unfurled
I smelled the hibiscus, the
Petal, the stamen, the stigma, the
Flower whole.
'Tis the hour to settle down
I surmised.

I slowed down my steps
Approached the shade on the
Bench less frequented.
Things moved at a measured pace
Gradually, by degrees.
The spider in its web suspended
Spun, the prey apprehended.
Now is the time
Lest it never arrives the
Ripened me the
Wrinkled I
Contentment writ all over.

THE JUNGLE BABBLER

There's this flock of jungle babblers
Often venturing into our territory as
Happened with others.
Six, seven or eight of them would group
One perched atop a high vantage point to
Keep guard the
Rest in restive mood
Hop, hopping with short flight bursts they would
Wake a dead soul out of slumber
Thus to say the
Cacophony thus compelling and loud
Not a day would pass
Without the shrill.
Of late, they are not to be seen
Thickets, groves having thinned out
As it is, there is enough of din
Adequate to drown the birds' note.
All this happened a decade back.
Saplings have taken root
Shrubs outgrown the
Jungle babblers are nowhere to be found

Near, far or around
Entertaining young and old alike
Perchance in distant land
With antics primeval, just, right.

THE FLYING MACHINE

The aircraft began its downward descent
From a heightened altitude of furthermore height
Gliding its way forward
Spatial vastness around.
With gradual progression
Later, much later
Could be discerned lights dimmed out
Lit pathways
Dark vegetative emptiness
Night surround.
The lights glowed lowering down
Brightened next
Megalopolis aglow.
A bump, some jerks for company
As the wheels rubbed the tarmac
The sound of rubber, metal runway
Giant machine technology unveiled
Steering clear of moist air
Insects and life forms
Drowned out by the deafening roar.
Aluminum marvel

Now stationed on firm ground
Stoic, resolute
Mission accomplished.

THANE CREEK

The creek lay bare to
Our right on the
Other hand as well a
Spread of grey waters
As far as could be seen
Lined by mangroves
Roots jutting out
All around to breathe, respire
Thrive in the brackish environs
Boasting of crabs, shrimps and
Crustaceans galore.
Gulls spiraled above
White and light
Wings spanned out
Now here and there, too
Feathers beaten and flapped in
Quick succession.
Country boats floated below
Few and sparse
Fishermen bedecked
Seeking the day's catch
Big, fat, rich yield

Abundant enough
Further down stood the flamboyance of flamingos
Slender, tall, pink.
Water flowed in
Water flowed out
Fluid expanse as
Distant as eyes could reach.
The creek still lay open
For the morrow
Day after
And the subsequent nights.

THE MARSHY WETLAND

Gentle ripples on the marsh
Surface borne from
Time immemorial
Regular routine fed to
Wind and breeze wed
Now glistened under the rays
Sun and moon thrived
Shaded dark, light
Yellow, red, crimson and white the
Changing moods
Days lengthened out
Now withdrawn
Huddled winter in vogue the
Wetland throbbed
Heaved and dropped
Webbed feet paddled
Swam ashore
Back afloat
Again and later in
Symphony synchronized
Pattern regularized
Daily henceforth in the

Lookout for
Duckweed and mollusks
Fish and crustacean
Water body shallow
Deep within
Blue and grey
Green hue
Moist, wet, aquatic delight
Smell of ducks, waterfowl at large
Submerged weeds
Aroused hope
Promising, bright.

THUS SHE FEATURED

The girl showed up.
It was a roll call
Their presence must
One March afternoon
Beneath the sun
Straight stood she
Face sweat and sodden
Eyes floating awhile in
Ceaseless restiveness by
Absence saddened
One she longed for
Long ago in
The past
The present mummified
She summed up courage and
Speak she did
At length
Old excepts
Moist tale
Rain bearing clouds and
Dense hail
Water drenched nights and

Disheveled selves
Braved it all the
Entire speech
Trodden path
Latent heat
Flung fancies and accumulated heap.
The girl did show up
In the face of it
Memory now faded
Erased deep.

CITY WEIGHED DOWN

The road winded up
Then down
Now spiraled above for
Leap unbound
Steered clear of edifices still
Life forms in motion
Movement, breath, respiration.
The vehicle of
Make sixties
Startled, in a fix
Downtown, city magnanimous
Metallic elements
Air weighed down
Laden heavy
Black, white, many more
Dark, dense
Toxic fumes all consumed
Mingled in shades of grey
Settled down upon foliage
Tree trunks hollow
Stout branches spread out.

Saddened men still marched
Down the road
Destination far
Hope nowhere around.
The road ran further
As did we
In the search
Resolute, unfailing
Yonder, beyond.

A MERE GARDEN

A small stretch of land it was
Into garden transformed
Flowering plants lining the periphery in
Full blossom
Verdant grass covered the earth a
Couple of trees here
Another pair there
Interspersed
Branches jutting out it
Woke up at dawn
With the sun
Along with the remnant dew
Earned nightlong
Stretching out in the daylight
Full yellow bright
Aerials naturalized
Daily chores with finesse executed
Pollen, sap
Gentle trickle
Resin and gum
Oozing withdrawn
Scattered fragrance

Scent abound
Dead log horizontal lay
Housing insects variegated
In moisture thrived
A small piece of land which was
Replenished, flourished
The task by no means small.

THE HOLY SURGE

Dim lit narrow alley
Holy men ochre fed
Flowers up for sale offered
Deity ancient divine
Way led to
Raised temple
Bells metal alloyed and
More of the kin
Hung heavy still but for the
Occasional strike
Sound reverberated down to the
Ear, mind all pervading
As did the conch shell
Deified form golden bright
Transfixed down the ages
Thus stood resplendent
Radiant wide round the
Pillars stout clay fed lime
Distant fortified unknown yet
White smoke arising camphor lit
Soothing upwards sandalwood and rose to
Erudite hymns, chants up close to

Jostle crowd thronged
Cleansed pious long longed
Loud gong further aloud
Time passed by space surround
Well lit narrow alley sun around
Rituals, rites, piety bound.

OF HARD DESCENT

I am a sculptor a
Stone carver chiseling
Statuettes out of sandstone in the
Floodplains a
Muddy hut to dwell in
Roof thatched slant wards
Leafy produce prosper in their
Midst me and my vocation
Now chipping away hard chips
Stony flakes
Grey brown granules into
Dust transform and
Down descend upon the
Clay containers, water pots
Sodden patch of earth
Today and all days
I act, toil and sweat out
Images taking shape in the mind
Then acquired by the stone mass
Dancing figurines, royal attendants
Deified forms, both heavily and
Scantily clad

Atop horses, on foot
Since age bygone
Practiced by our clan
Mere mortals but the
Frozen works remain for
Posterity to behold
Some banal, commonplace
A little few striking bold
Like the one across
Two thousand three hundred years old.

SUGARCANE CRUSH

The cart lay stationed
Four small wheels rubberized for
Smooth passage down the street
Some wood, some iron
Into the making went.
Dark brown sugarcane
Heaps of them
Piled one above the other
Some peeled to make way for
Juicy extract
Mint flavored lime admixture
Which outcome through the
Device paired
Rotating cylinders crushing
Yellow and white readied canes
Oozing nectar mellow sweet in
Earthen tumblers poured
Iced and not
As you please to
Satiate thirst
Parched indeed.
Men of all make thronged

So did the bees
Smell overpowering of
God's own creation
Pleasant, full of flavor
Noble designs
Joy pure, discreet.

OF HUMAN SUBJUGATION

Would you come out with me
Past lanes, streets, roads and
Lead us to the garden recluse
Tucked away far
Across and across
On to the pathways
Charted out on purpose for
Us to saunter, reflect and ponder
Amidst trees, shrubs and
Grass green the
Lake small
Bubbling keen on
Evenings duskier than
You, me to
Dim lit lamps
Victorian by Queen's decree.
Night advanced, stridulating
Crickets sound
All around
Broken by a screeching owl or a
Nightjar, unknown, unseen
Frightening one to the bench

Firm, wide, clean to
Normalcy back with the
Advent of stars
Blue, innumerable
Set against the black screen
Or the fireflies enlightened
Down below
Red, orange, yellow.
Would you come out with me
Afresh, on other occasions the
Countenance and hue
Like the morning dew and
Make miracles of dreams
Smashing inhibitions, bodily, umpteen.

DEAD SPARKLE

The steps led down to the river
Placid, silent
Laid back still
Flowing further east and
Southwards as well
Dense, carrying gallons of water
Below, underneath
Above which floated
Country boats ready to
Cater to tourists, visitors
Pilgrims few
Past structures medieval dotted on the
Banks, alongside
Piled up wooden logs
Slit loose to arouse flames on
Funeral pyres heaped behind to the
Accompaniment of wails
Smelling flesh
Burnt up, charred in the
Fire and its throes
Gulls white encircling the distant end
Grey and dark

Evening now descends down the
River black brightened by
Dead sparks illuminating us alive.

THE BUS HAS DEPARTED

I had that omnibus of mine
Painted red of
Tin make full of
Passengers seated alongside windows
Square open to the world outside
Within the driver at the helm and the
Conductor issuing tickets and
Off it went with a bump
Advancing down ahead by
Manual maneuvers which I undertook
Plastic wheels improvised coming to my aid
Day and night to
Joyous moments
Long forgotten.
As far as my memory served a
Sheet of metal it was
Beaten to shape and then
Images drawn
Faces pressed against the apertures
Still, silent sight

Frozen further by intervening decades
Receding into oblivion
Distant, lonely, quiet.

REASON AND RHYME

The house her housed
White and grey
The flames couldn't be doused
Still in the fray
Pretty isn't she
Bright aflame
Honey and bee
Immaculate dame
Smooth swayed the palm
Tall above
Soothing balm
Cooing dove
Household chores
Regular accomplished
Within and outdoors
Timely unleashed
The passage of day
Scented flowers
Couldn't keep me at bay
Long hours
The sight, the smell
The sound hushed up

Did verily me ail
To dine, to sup
To ask her out
Past mellow fields
Infatuation devout
Magic yields
To soar, to glide
To swim beneath
To call out, to hide
To startle on heath
Grin, smile, laugh aloud
Jump, bump, out tire
And lead her safe as vowed
Innocence writ, no quagmire
Pink clouds, slant rays
Cooler surround
Yellow maize
Barb wire hound
Her abode neared
Faintly clear
No longer weird
Cherished and dear
The house would her house
Pure sublime
Thoughts noble arouse
And further my rhyme.

FADED ACQUAINTANCE

Acquaintance at work
One crazy the
Other fashion led
Execute his job the
Other her design
Had designs, too, he
On further proximity
Smiles, exchange of words
Past produce, products
Material raw and hide.
Days passed by
Weeks accumulated on
Respect befitting
Mutually reciprocated rightfully theirs a
Commoner he
Of regal descent she
Though admiration up stirred for
Him and her
Met never again
Compulsions galore
This tale of yore
Of his and yours

Of norms and strictures
Past laid down
Rigorous throughout
Country and town
To keep at bay
Wishes long cherished
Far, away.

HARSH WINTER

A cold winter evening
Bereft of power
Had me reclined around the fireplace
One across the other
It was then that I
Lighted the gas stove
Poured water into the kettle
Placed it atop
Sprinkled some tea leaves
Let it boil
Steam gushing out of the spout the
Lid dancing the
Conifer against the window shook
Actually the branches.
It was a frozen, barren day
All I could make out was
Silhouettes dark and darker
The cold winter evening
Overpowered further
Still, lonely, aghast.

There was no human form around the
Silence broken
By an intermittent distant howl.

QUAIL TALE

There was this group of quails
Four, five, maybe six of them
Small striated brown
Walking, one behind the other on
Firm ground, dry vegetative growth on a
Winter morning
As is wont
I spotted another twosome
Mellow sun overhead and a
Singular of the species on the
Dry hills
On a different occasion.
Now this piece of barren tract
Adjacent to the farm land had
Sported quails times without number
Little endearing ones
Perfectly camouflaged
Against the setting
Full replete
Enjoying nature's bounty
Passerby few with

No one to startle them out from their
Planet wonderful
Imagery complete.

THE STREET MAGICIAN

Our childhood saw this magician on the street
Who would amass crowd
Circular encircling him
Displaying antics old forgotten
Like the one wherein he would
Gulp down two, three iron spheres the
Size of oranges, ferrous, dark and
Regurgitate those, one by one or the
One which had him juggle with
Four balls at one go.
Then there was a trick more severe
When a person would lie down still and
Rise up positioned fully horizontal to the road and
You could see clear crystal like
Nothing absolutely beneath to
Hold him aloft
High above the ground.
We would stand in awe of his
Spells, magical to say the least.
I do not if it all was
Feigned, fictitious, illusive but it did

Make one believe in the illusory illusion the
Belief that magic had happened that
We were subject to it and
Now when things appear dull and drab
More often than not and
Monotonous, too
I do wish and hope
Hoping against hope that
Someone alike turns up and
Turns the tables to
Wide applause resonant and
Tumultuous upheaval.

THE SPOTTED OWLET

In the dead tree trunk
Lay nestled spotted owlets
Two of them
Mottled past recognition
Could not have asked for a better camouflage
Merged into the surrounding
Wood light
Would hunt in the dark
Mice, lizards, small rodents
Whatever they could lay their hands on
Claws, talons in fact
Sharp, incisive, swooping down and
Pouncing on the prey with
Precision unseen, unheard of, the
Wingspan much too wide for the
Small sized owls
When back to their arboreal cavities would
Hold the prey intact and
Pierce open the body, the
Flesh with the beak a
Delicious sumptuous meal
Well worth the toil.

All this happened after dark
As also the calls vocalized
Emanating at intervals specified.
These spotted owlets still
Inhabit the weathered tree the
Mysterious haunt imparting
Color and diversity
To listless forms and humanity
For us
As well as posterity.

THE APPLE HUNT

That summer the hotel
We had put up in
Boasted of an apple orchard
Plantation all around
Needless to say
Laden with red ripe ones
Ready to be plucked.
We as children would
Hurl our shoes for
Want of an apt missile
Aiming the apples and lo
One or twice as many would
Verily land on the stretch of grass
After much ado.
Hens and roosters would forage
Looking for dropped fruit and
Peck those unto oblivion.
We, too, on our part
Would not lag behind and
Devour the fruit of our labor with
Devotion utmost and discreet

Ways and means devised.
That's all about the apples
That's all about the orchard
The hunt, the capture
And the execution.

THE SCARECROW

A vertical twig stuck in the ground a
Smaller horizontal one tied
Slightly above midway served as
Arms straw struck the
Vertical one spoken of earlier
Served as legs and body proper a
Torn shirt clad an
Earthen pot made up for the
Head, face, eyes, teeth
All painted casually, rough strokes.
A scarecrow it was weather beaten
Stood in the sun
Drenched itself in the rains
Swayed to the right, the left
At the mercy of gusts of wind had
Hair none
Brown clay and hay
Wore a wide grin always to
Serve a purpose to
Scare away birds and
Act sentinel to the

Surrounding cobs
Golden, yellow replete
Furnishing yield mature, complete
While the crows, sparrows it robs.

PRISTINE GLORY

The drizzle having subsided the
Road ahead lay black washed
Puddles of rainwater and an
Occasional passing vehicle of which
One had oil droplets
Dropping down the way the
Color of oil on thin films
Bright, resplendent
Contracting now, dilating next as
Brilliant it could get the
Neighboring clear pools reflecting the
Near-blue sky, the fluffy white clouds
Shadows cast by two passersby and
My own reflection weather beaten
Now water splashed.
I heaved a sigh of relief
So close leaning down as would
Create ripples
Pristine, pure.

THE CHEMICAL ME

I made good my entry into the Chemistry laboratory
Elements and compounds in
Solid and liquid state
I gazed at the bottles, pipette, burette the
Jars, wire gauze, Bunsen burner the
Oceanic blue of copper sulfate the
Pungent gaseous hydrogen sulfide
Custom made the
Much too intense bromine gas the
Rings circular rising up
Wavering, undulating and into the
Formless air would it merge and
Then vanish.
Not that I did not conduct a
Few experiments of my own a
Chemist in the offing
Creating meanwhile
Effervescence, sparks and
Some fireworks
For posterity to decipher.

WHEN THE KNICKERBOCKERS HELD SWAY

I had a pair of knickerbockers of
Blue thick cotton weave a
Couple of pocket sideways to
Store marbles, lozenges and
All I could lay my little hands on a
Few buttons bulbous to button up
Stout intact
My daily ordeals
Sporting pride, contentment
Comfort in addition which
Shone under the sun
Wettened in the drizzle, the rain the
Downpour intense then
Assumed a stiff dry demeanor the
Next morn, blaze overhead.
It reigned supreme
As did I
Until a barbed wire fence
Ripped it apart.

I contracted a few bruises
It did hurt
Not so much for the wound
As for the shattered view of the
Knickers in tatters
Pathos writ all over.

FOOTBALL

Now that the football has been inflated
It's ready to jump, bump to
Endure headers, kicks to
Crash against the goalpost to
Whizz past the goalkeeper
Get entangled in the net to be
Flung afar throw struck to be
Dribbled past defenders to be
Hand held for a sin to be committed a
Foul act to be
Swerved like a banana kick and
All of these and more to
Impart joy and pleasure much awaited to
Packed stands, crowded stadiums
Reverberating with thunderous applause the
Antics down below displayed by the
Sportive opponents on the field
Thanks to this rotund friend of ours
Hide and leather all compact.

OUR WOODEN SLED

The wooden sled of ours
Well, it was rented
Stood us in good stead
We slid downhill
Snow accumulated over days
Wet, white all this while
We did get stuck the
Gradient not steep enough
With some fuss did manage to
Advance further down the slope
There were others around
Fur lined woolens and yaks
Massive, hirsute
Black and white
Calm, composed ready to
Cater to the needs.
The pines, the cones the
Distant waterfall, the rumble
All bode us well.
This wooden sled of ours
This transportation of yore

Pierced through chunks of ice
Massive enough to
Offer us views further
Betterment one over the other.

AND THE CATERPILLAR GROW UP

A multi colored caterpillar it was
Black, green, yellow, red
Devouring thick milkweed leaves
Throughout the day
As well as night I suppose
For what could be seen the subsequent mornings
Elongated meanwhile
For it had to grow and outgrow
Then to cocoon transform and
Attain the status of a butterfly but
Before that it had to had its
Abdomen full to
Absorb all the goodness
All the nutrients which the
Milkweed possessed to pass to its
Aerial hover to
Take to flight to
Get its intake of nectar and
Dance to the cosmic rhythm
Thus ordained.

NO MORE UNSUNG

It is pretty hard initially
As if you are out in the open sea.
However much you are prepared the
Ground reality is altogether different.
Nowadays, in fact, during the last couple of decades
You have more access to aids
Thanks to the technical advancements.
Instead of groping in the dark
You look out for help in the twilight.
You might as well get scorned or scoffed at but
With the passage of time
With the graying of hair
Having had to translate more texts it
Tends to be your second nature.
Now you can steer through
Of course with some jerks and bumps in the offing
As accompaniment.
Memorable moments there aren't too many but
Yes, a word of praise a
Laid back nod an

Endearing glance
Although a rarity
Makes your day.

UNKNOWN

Dense green trees
Fruit laden
Hung low
Barely touching the ground
Dark foliage at dusk
In the twilight zone
Turning olive
Then military green shaded
In no while thick, opaque
Not to be penetrated the
Head is dizzy
Dazed, aghast
Silence, much too often
Broken by the flowing river
Ripples, some waves
Liquid, fluid
Gliding past
Still, firmly rooted trees
Brown branches
Browner trunk
Vacuum pervades

Void round, circular, spherical
Now rotating
Then revolving anew
In concentric circles
Cold unknown.

THE RATTLE

The metal rattle sounded not
Until it shook
Shaken by tiny hands
Gentle jerks
Now and then and
There you could hear the ring the
Beat diminishing far and wide
As much as the room
Could make room
For tinted pink and purple
On the silver body
Shining with the onset
Of the sun, the sunset
And bright lit full moon nights
Descending down upon us every month
Some more intense than the rest
Not very melodious, though the
Rattle did instill some rhythm a
Flow, waves pink and purple
True to the shades
Radiating brilliance
Brilliant celestial glow.

MIGHTIEST MIGHT

Not that you would have been overrun
By the speeding train but the
Air whistle with wide repercussions
Waves overlapping one another and
Into the eardrum the
Impending speed the
Metallic monster whizzing past the
Massive solid metallic mass the
Sheer proportion could outweigh the
Mightiest among the mighty
You, me, he, she
So did we
Hand held in hand
Crossing the railway tracks
Trembling in unison with the
Ferrous tremble in the tracks
Sweating in tandem with the
Moist air gushed up by the locomotive
As the world was in turmoil
Ours, yours and who knows whose
In the tropical country settlement
Distant flickering lights a

Pyre lit aglow
Fire in full swing
Heaving, panting
Gasping afresh.

THE PULLED SUGAR MAN

And the man would go around the
Lanes and by lanes
Selling his ware.
Yes, he is the pulled sugar man or
Rather, the seller
Wound around a wooden staff brown
Displaying colors
White striated red, green and
What not
Sweetened a way bit more than
We could but make we did
On days bright, sunny or
Contrary otherwise.
Did not cost much
Except the long wait
Past noon according to the
Whims and fancies
Not ours but the
Oft-repeated, fabled
Pulled sugar seller of yore

Now stationed deep inside the
Minds of whomsoever it had concerned
Sweetened beyond recognition.

JASMINE IN BLOOM

White tubular jasmine
Sprouting forth with
Spontaneous ease on
Star lit nights
Still, silence broken by
Crickets in chirp
Incessant, unceasing
Consummate, if you please.
The night, as is wont
Dark, black
Blue lit above
High, high up at a
Distance distant
Far away.
Other flowers emanate
Smell, sweet intoxicating odor
Out of the world
Fit for angels, cherubs
Men and women true
Pure, sublime.
The tubular jasmine still blooms

As do the other flowers on
Star lit nights
Fresh, tender
Wrought in marvel wonder.

THE MAN WHO GREW YOUNG

This is a story
Obviously not true
Of a man
Who grew young with age
Shed a tummy
Of which he had little
Felt rejuvenated
By degrees augmented
As days passed by
Yet to reach its zenith
Perplexed by the changes bodily
From abysmal depths arose to
Heightened glory
Comprehend he could little the
Prying eyes, the
Prodding folks
Men inquisitive
Looking at askance
Posing questions
Queer, weird

Far removed from the ordinary
The man grew
Drew upon the days gone by the
Bygone nights the
Obvious acquaintance
Chance meetings
Mind, matter, the quaint neighborhood
How it stifled
How he perspired
Seeking intervention cosmic, diabolic, divine.

NESTING TERMITES

The termites, after much ado
Did construct a nest on
Earthen mound
Hardened to withstand the
Vagaries of nature the
Termites within
Hordes of them
Colonies abound
Would swarm all over
Intricate tunnels
Pathways labyrinthine
Wherein to grow in number
Teeming multitude
Theirs of a kind to
Serve a purpose
Existential, exponential
Soaring high in their order
As ordained
Chewing all awhile
Brownish brown winged wonder.

LONG PLUCKED

Garlands up for sale
Strung out of marigold
Yellow, orange, reddish brown tinged
Close to the city square
Just across the tallest spire
Where the temple rose high
Instilling faith amongst one and all
Draped in fragrance fresh the
Floral dangle from up atop
Hung loose
Brushing the paved pathway in
Small measure the
Odor swinging across on
Windswept days and
On still fragrant morn
Taut intact the
Smell frozen with no
Signs of dispersal
Glum, crestfallen flowers
Long plucked far away.

AS IS WONT

I have been doing this for years
Waking up, eating
Sitting, walking, sleeping
And rising up again the
Next morn
As is wont.
It all started one fine day in the
Middle of the century went by
I suppose
Amid profusely scented flowers
Dew struck
Fluffy white clouds
Later, much later afterwards
Night, twilight fed
Dark, further intense
Blackened beyond recognition.
All this has been happening
Over the decades on the
Planet earth
Now scarce, next abundant in
Tumultuous upheaval to
Thunderous applause.

ORANGE MARMALADE

After much ado
Bustle and din subsided
Lid unsettled
Off came revealing this
Bittersweet smell
Color orange thick, viscous
Marmalade-like.
Well, it's orange marmalade
Prepared with care discreet
Out of ripe mellow oranges in
Some quaint country orchard
Far removed miles further the
Odor much too maddening
So as to attract you, me and them
One bright sunny morning
Ripe and luscious
Pulp, rind the
Aroma, ours forever.

THE SILENT COSMOS

It lay barren for ages
Hard brown rock
Crevices and fissures
Must have borne the brunt in
Sweltering heat
Under the sun scorched
Out of contention
For days without number
Incessant, this wondrous patch of earth
Stagnant, still, mummified
Gait stoic, composed
Spreading out as far as
Could meet the eye
Farther than the distant horizon
Now blue
Now crimson silence pervades
Twilight approaching
Meandering through the
Color purple
Trickling down the finest pore.

HINDI PARK

And the road led to Hindi Park
Adorned with
White concrete mushrooms
Structured to provide shade the
Sun nearing completion
Somewhere around
Hot, bright yellow
As was the marigold in
Clustered order
Papaya springing green, lean
Red scented rose
Margosa bitter sweet to
Blades of grass
Dense unkempt beyond summer in the
Rain flowing past down away
Having trickled down the wet flowers
Bathed leaves
Moist twigs, branches, stems
Trunk submerged to
Croaking frogs in full- throated ease
Grey, yellow, green

Swimming in accompaniment
Legs outstretched
Hopping on bare stretches, if any.
Rains subsided
Flowers galore
To this day profuse, intense.

THIS LAMP OF MINE

It's my spherical lamp
Which shines bright in the
Darkest night
Shaded vitreous to
Etchings marked out with
Human images
Men, women and the like
Offering solace
Dispelling doubts
Growing in stature
Day in and out
Frightening away hours
Ill-equipped, disliked
Lit aglow to illumine
Hearts and minds of the
Teeming millions
Inclusive of You and I.

THE ONION SELLER

It's dusk
Time for the kohl laden seller to
Display the ware
Spread out uneven on the cart, undulating
Purple red
Flowing Indian attire, mirrored
By bare thread sewn onto
Reflecting the world passing by
Time unwinding, unleashed
Men frequenting
Women as much
Juveniles adding to the din
As is the case with
Bazaars bizarre, earthly
Old world at the foothills
Beneath the shaded rock
Hot winds subsided
It is time for some breeze
Cool to say the least
Blowing past crevices discreet
Rickety wooden wheels

Horses and mules
Onto the face kohl-smeared
Oriental haired
Trying to invoke in vain the
Buying spree.

THE SCHEME OF THINGS

The window lay spread
One fresh autumnal morning
Jutting out onto the fall views
As would be offered to the
Discerning few with
Creeper intertwined
Climbing up to the tallest vine
Squirrel-like
Acorns and nuts to be munched
Others dropped further down on the
Land black brown
Dew-fed leaves for
Mollusks to thrive upon
Thawed, still, time stood stagnant
But for the early breeze a
Slight flutter, flapping of wings a
Shriek call a
Note shrill
Head bobbing up and down
Beak in drill
Half-eaten fruits by

Flying fox fed to
Fruition led
Dropped feathers, plumes few
Holes pecked deep for
Grubs and worms
Amid plants and animals the
Kingdoms in unison wed.

THE JEWEL BUG

Scaling high the upright twig
The bug shone bright
With all its might
Sphere halved rotund and big
Lying there awhile
All iridescent
One entire crescent
In its rank and file
Intermittent illumines
Radiating light
Heavenly sight
Thereupon out weans
Greenish blue
Bluish green
Colors umpteen
Dazzling hue
Ruddy red
Saffron orange
Copious range
By angels fed
Cherubs' hug

Bejeweled wonder
To applause thunder
This jewel bug.

THE PRAYING MANTIS

The mantis clasped still the
Bare stem colored brown
Much like itself
Rufus tawny
Forelegs folded akin
Thorax perpendicular
As grew the plant
Abdomen lying in wait
For its prey
How it prayed to
Begin with its day's catch to
Devour to its full
Succulent insects or
Those with a crunch
Bulbous eyes protruding out
Head moving sideways
Swaying all awhile
Trying to decipher to
Gauge how far
How distant away
Kept it at bay
And in small degrees having neared

Pounce it will in no time
Escape nowhere to be found
This then earmarked the onset
Devastating for one
For some triumphant
Sealing the other's fate.

DESERT BOUND

It is near-desert zone
Semi-arid, dry
Spiny thorns, some flower bedecked
Violet, yellow pistil
Stamen the same coloration
Rocks underneath protruding above
Lending the path uneven
Hard to the core.
A horned lizard peeps out
Licking thick black ants
Its abdomen full a
Pall of dust envelops
Swaying, gliding past
Settling down soft, gentle
Upon granules, pebbles the
Earth below tawny
Rufus in part
Springs above acacia in bloom
Pointed sharp, incisive the
Leaves endearing themselves unto
Dromedary rustic now
Bobbing up and down the

Lick, the munch, the
Tongue out appears
All in tandem
As does the sun
Over the hillock parched
Pouring itself out
In this very terrain
Verily hot, perspiring day
Panting
And yet more.

ON VIEWING A LILY POND

The water lilies upright stood
In the pond placid
Silent, still water
Pink, white, yellowish
Skywards projecting
Roots down beneath in the
Muddy interior the
Shallow bottom unclear
Spreading all throughout
As far as could meet the eye
Round leaves circular in fashion
Extended flat atop the liquid medium
Green, very green
Rich green, in fact
Flowers, anther attracting
Bees, dragonflies, brethren aerial
Hovering and gliding well past
Encircling circuitous
Red, orange, yellow fliers
Wings outstretched floating
Lie submerged you, me
Resplendent colors for company.

IT RAINED THAT DAY

It caught me unaware
Did it drizzle?
It was plain downpour
Rain pouring down from above
With no discernible shade
Drenching me in completion
In no time reigned the liquid cold
Chill moving down my spine
Afflicted with fright
Not a living soul in sight
View blinded
Shooting rain downwards
In unison all
Gathered might
I pulled ahead
With hardship much a
Rain fed being
Washed away
Past thunder, clouds the
Bustle and din.

THE DARK ACT

Dark, air-cooled
Could fairly be discerned
Rows of seats
Vacuous, empty the
Stage occupied by us a
Handful few
All decked up for the act
Enactment real the
Days numbered
While today we rehearse
As is the wont
All these yesteryears
Past, silent the
Silence broken by
Whispers or murmurs anew to
Disheveled hair, carefully undid or
Plaits brown, swaying braids.
Readying ourselves by gradual degrees
Perform we did to
Eyes, paired all
Hidden, black, obsolete.

GEARING UP FOR CHILDHOOD

When you have attained
All of six years or
One more in excess
On the way to school the
Teacher accompanies you
With care utmost, discreet
When you are carefree
In safe hands
Trot and gallop
Wherever you find your way through
When you spring up
Early in the morning
Pillows, crumpled up bed sheet a
Rickety cot
When you dance to the blooming flower
When you run after the floating spores
Popped off by ripened pods
Yellowed, mellowed, full to the seam
When you hum, sing, fret and cry
Under open skies

When you run after peewit
I mean land plover
Those red wattle lapwing fledglings
When you yearn for all of these
Over and over again
You are let loose
A child
Soaring high for fun and frolic
Soft, gentle, mild.

OLD SCHOOL

The staircase spiraled up
Black, of iron formed
As high as my neck could it strain a
Couple of feet or more
Above the paved floor
Adjoining the outlet selling
Potatoes baked and hot
Sprinkled with spices normal
Banal, commonplace the
Smell lingering on still, flowing
Encircling the senses distant
Far, further away
Rose above the ferrous erect
Circuitous, whirlwind-like to
Nowhere atop
As could conjure the impish lot
Down below
On hard ground the
Fire fed stove, the blue flames
Steam vapor surround
Moist and dampening.

AND THE MUSIC TOOK ROOT

The room housed musical instruments
Sans players
None who could strum the string or
Thump the drum or
Better still blow the pipe a
Flute shining, dark
Black to the brim
If it could be said such the
Clarinet, the tambourine
Cymbals bright steel
Silver glitter
On second gaze still brighter
Lay still, silent
Reclining against the calcareous wall
Some held upright
Straightened wooden cases
Dissipating aroma straight out of
Arboreal turpentine.

ON CATCHING A GLIMPSE OF ARABIAN SEA

The sea heaved and
Splashed and tossed the
Saline water out in the
Liquid mass
Like it had done for ages
Since time immemorial the
Fishing boats undulated
Upon the waves set in motion
Perpetual swaying live in the
Sea Arabic windy warm
Yachts dazzling white swam past
Making the most of a day
Unleashed, blowing west
Merging in the stillness spread wide
Way beyond the farthest horizon
Maddening reckless, unruly
Unbound.

THE PEAFOWL VISIT

The first thing to catch my eye in the
Morning subsequent to the
Preceding night was the
Peafowl blue
Greenish, too, strutting around the
Balcony square beside our room
Vitreous, transparent through the
Tail feathers brushing objects two the
Table round, marble laid the
Ebony chair, black, true
Out in the open air fed
Fresh born
This very morn
Unlike the peacock which added
Years few
Youthful grace
Flown this end from the
Scrubland with trees interspersed the
Remaining lot on firm ground
Terrestrial, yet more arboreal, few.

FISH BEING UP FOR SALE

Fisherwomen many, more
Hordes of them
Walked past the still town the
March breaking the silence
Footsteps, way forward
Pulled on from behind
Cane baskets balanced just on
Heads popping and swaying to
Keep at bay contents
Containers added to the
Woe weighing down the
Path arduous, distant long
Till the destination reached
Attaining contentment multi-hued
Now a smile, a giggle a
Laughter more often than not
Hitherto sparse sale commenced
Jingling coins, soiled currency the
Smell of fish, crustaceans white
Silver glitter, jaws held wide.

GOPALPUR BOAT

It's a boat
Washed ashore on the
Hotel grounds
Facing the mighty sea the
Wooden one lying upturned
Keel, some iron
Dried, weather-beaten
Exposing the furious might
Unleashed the fateful day
Earmarked for devastation the
Boatman missing
Annihilated by Nature's wrath the
Swirl, the upheaval
Tossed and flung afar
For us to dwell upon
Then lament the passing away
Fading into far removed oblivion
Distant
Drowned by the seas.

FOOD FOR THE SOUL

Who all the frequent the restaurant
Close to the causeway a
Lane or two apart in
Operation for decades
Lost count of
Set afar by days bygone
Old, decrepit structure now
Falling if not on the
Verge at least
Serving rice, fish curry, chicken
Pork vindaloo and
Dishes more in ceramic bound and
Plates scratched upon by hungry souls and
Fingers, inquisitive few to the
Chiming of bell
Metallic, heavy of
Dark hue.

SCHOOL PICNIC

I am queued up to
Board the bus of
Leyland make
Thus to make amends for the
Days lost to studies
Relevant or not and
Alight I would
My lunch clasped tight
Packed full and wide
Alongside the seat assigned the
Window around
Bus set in motion past
City streets, roads, marts
Trade commenced
Faces glum, swelling crowds and
Out in the open
Garden green, lush, verdant
Smelling of leaves, flowers, nectar of
Earth moist, wet anew
Sound of whizzing bees
Flutter of wings
Call of birds unknown, unheard of

Flap of black kites
Swooping down for the
Catch, our prized possession
Delicacies one or few a
Day bright, resplendent
Sun above, at its zenith
Golden, mellow
Sweet discrete.

LIVE FROM THE CITY

I mean
They mean business
City swung into action
Briefcases black gliding past
Others of their brethren
One out weaning the next to
Reach its destination
Destined, pre-destined
Mere mortals we
Running helter-skelter
Bus loads of men
Scores of them or
Maybe hundreds or
In thousands in
Brownian motion set
Zigzag, circular and
All possible movements
Yearning for the unknown.

ONCE UPON A TIME

And the room resounded
Claps, rhymes, melodious few
Below decorated ceiling, chandelier strung
Weighing down
Silver glitter, a flash of light
Food being served, clinking glasses
Fragrance state-of-the-art
Custom spread, just right for the
Occasion, partying men and wives of
Tales forgotten
Dug out from memory
Curtains drawn, pulled blinds of
Pine or otherwise
Reflecting past glory in the
Belgian mirror ornate, floral
Larger than life.

THE STAGE IS SET

It's red hot earth
Crystallized, granular rather
Coarsely settled around the bay
Nurturing scantily clad trees and
Reptiles few, and still fewer
Close to the upward cliff a
Shallow descent downwards to the
Blue expanse
Miles of it, unfathomable, too, in
All its grandeur
Not far from the hard ground
Solid land exercising
Firm hold on the roots
Pierced deep within
Clasping and sustaining the animal kingdom
All this while.

THE JACKFRUIT TREE

The jackfruit tree
Green and brown
Laden heavy
Stood upright the
Fruit turned half yellow
Now yellowish black
Ripe to the core
Spread fragrance
Emanating all this while the
Mature produce
Ready to be plucked and
Devoured to the full
Fulfilling its purpose of
Demonstrating
Another of Nature's wonders.

DIFFICULT QUITE

With lot of difficulty
Hard strive, do I contrive
Words in sequence right
Such was to be my plight
When fancy would take to flight
Making giant strides
Leaving me desperate in
Poor light to
Fend for myself the
Battle of mind over mindlessness of
Arduous labor of
Erudition bright to
Frame phrases to
Coin lines fit for
Eternity to remember
Reminisce, quiet.

IN THE MANGROVES

I am in mangrove land a
Delta so large
As match could none
Trees with roots
Out protruding to inhale air the
Red crabs in
Activity diurnal the
Wild boar and hyena in hiding to
Disclose themselves
Under darkness.
Eerie silence pervades
Broken by intermittent crickets
Stridulating aloud
Splash of distant waves on
Shores, beaches, mudflats
Birds yet to take off
For the day
Sun still marked a
Monitor lizard slides its way
Through muddy banks
Crabs entangled in the roots

Half submerged
Twisted and gnarled
There's a sudden disturbance
In the water in a
Flash it disappears a
Reptile I surmise
Danger being far removed a
Flick of the tongue the
Lightning bite.

HUMANKIND

In the nothingness the
Vacuous void pervades
You, Me the
Populace populating the sphere
I glide and sit atop a peak
Pointed rock, liverwort and
Some moss green
Swooping down below
As would frighten the spirit a
Spirited effort, energetic maneuvers in a
Pensive mood, hand resting
Against the chin
Contemplating what went awry
What could have been bettered upon
Non-existential, to mortality doomed the
Sound emanating, the din down under
Pretty faces, passionate glow a
Furtive glance, sweet, mellow
My senses are all awake
Hair raised, goose bumps few
Failures all, achievements new the

Great divide, disparity further
Enclosed, increased manifold.
It's cold above the
Chill thrives
Water droplets hazy
Opaque, unclear
Likened to our lives hitherto in
Meadows and vales
Isles isolated or
Boroughs and lanes
To what avail
All in vain.

HORSES IN THE STABLE

Now there's this horse stable and
Mules few un carted
Fodder fed, groomed to
Let loose their worries the
Toil anew, unbridled
Horse buns littered around the
Equine smell settles down
Neighs, swishing tails
Flowing manes
Hooves being dealt with
Taken good care of
Carts placed upright the
Cleaning commences
Whipping up the odor
Strong, typical
Characteristic of sheer strength and
Power
Muscular, raring to go
It's horse power.

FELINE FELICITY

It's nothing unique
Simply a feline quartet
Four cats occupying the city pavement
In and out they would move the
Turnstile facilitating the movement
Stealthy, wary of what all goes around the
Whiskers coming to the aid of the
Black one, jet black, in fact
Tawny striated the
One Banded grey the
Dappled brown cat completes it a
Rat, a mouse would suffice
So would the leftover delicacies
From the neighborhood or
Milk, spilled or otherwise
Would mew, purr, lick the paws
Eyes brightening by the night the
Cat's eye a
Gem in its own right.

IT'S ONLY A STORY

I still recollect the
One-eyed monster
Running with a boulder held high to
Hurl it at passing boats and
Drown those a
Story it was but
When your innocence gets the
Better of you
Tend to believe the
Horror, the shriek the
Pain, agony, turmoil so
Intense as could turn
Stranger than truth
Waking us out of our slumber to
Counter the Unknown the
Unseen.

CITY SUPREME

The city palatial
Palaces erected last century and
Earlier still
Offered magnificent views
Wherever one could set
One's eyes on the
Regal splendor the
Tree-lined avenues
Gardens laid in geometrical pattern
Channels water-fed leading to fountains
Statues installed at public squares of
Kings and queens
Men and women of royal descent
Steep ascent
Led to a garden
Overlooking the bay
Massive trees grown old with age
Gnarled, twisted
Spread far and wide the
Branches flung in directions all
Iron furniture laid out for

Us to relax, repose and recline to the
Sound of siren out far the
Occasional bird calling out or
Shrieking shrill
Perchance to emperors and monarch who
Once ruled supreme.

WALKING INTO DARKNESS

Having disembarked the train
I leave the station
Walking past files of rickshaws and
Others piled one upon the other in
Heaps, the wreckage
Leads to shops selling fritters
Smell of oil heated up the
Splashing sound of the release and the
Subsequent aroma
I walk and walk
Alongside water bodies and the
Occasional swamp the
Marsh teeming with life
Further ahead are country folks and
Hawkers few
Paddy and rice fields
Bamboo thickets cricket embedded to
Break the eerie silence a
Store of rural make is
Selling tea, piping hot
With basil and cardamom replete.

It's time for dusk to set in
I am in no hurry
In no time it's going to be dark
Blackness enhanced by fireflies
Found here in abundance rich the
Magic has begun the
Scent is profuse the
Screech nears
As does the distant howl.

AND THEN IT VANISHED

And then it vanished in
Thin air under clear skies
You remember as do I the
Association, getting associated
Enraptured, the enthrall
Second to none the
Melody, rhapsody pronounced the
Gentle fall, soft, light, ethereal
As the sun did pierce grey clouds
One overcast day but
If for a moment
Fleeting joy, never lasting
Away did fly
One gloomy afternoon
Rain commenced the previous evening
Still in possession the
Day in succession
Fat drops, piercing cold and
Then it vanished.

MY FIRST LIBRARY

A metallic trunk it was
Housing books for children
Relating tales, fables
Fairies and demons
Elves and goblins
Their travails
All that they encountered
Which when opened
Revealed a kingdom of opportunities
Things plausible as well as
Never to be the
Very first library it was
Books piled one atop the other in
Some order, though the
Unfolding of the spectacle a
Gasp of breath, a sigh
Contentment galore.

THE SNAKE CHARMER

The snake charmer an
Entity much too common in
This part of the globe is
No more to be seen the
Loose attire the
Turban wrapped atop
Bag load of snakes
Cobra, I was given to believe
Swaying to the wind instrument
Being played in
Narrow lanes and street corners
Entertaining us in our infancy
Childhood and adolescence the
Serpent keeping an eye on the
Instrument movement
Sweeping us off our feet
Involving admiration in
Awe, wonder-struck
At the performing duo
One outwitting the other.

THE POOR PUPPET

The puppet having escaped was all alone the
Master having left for the day a
Thin streak of light filtered in
Wasn't enough to make out things in the dark
Grope it would and stumble upon
Rising again to explore on foot
Having spent all its life in the box
Packed to perfection the
Wooden body, in geometric pattern
Did advance
Knees, elbows, joints the
Head, all in motion
Trying to make out the new realm the
Odor, the fragrance the
Slight murmur or the
Advancing footsteps.
Someone's knocking at the door.
It's all over.

DARKNESS AGAIN

It's a dark evening
Trees large and stout
Lined the path desolate
No one to be found
Except the fragrance of
Oriental flowers in bloom
Intensifying by degrees or in
Leaps and bounds
Night sky boasting stars
Blue, bluish, whitish blue
Set high above
Higher than the highest stratum
There's a gentle breeze blowing the
Nightjar calls out the
Owl hoots.
I wasn't vociferous enough.
Silence pervades.
Silent, placid, calm.

BLACK KITES

Did you notice the black kites
Playfully circling the skies
Uneven circles they were.
One morning, two of those were
Spotted atop the oak tree in the
Nest alongside a couple of
Fledglings, chicks hatched the
Other day, trying to feed them with
Fish bright, caught live
From the sea down below the
Kites called out loud
Somewhat resembling a horse's neigh the
Feathers ruffled in the breeze above the
Sharp beak curved downwards the
Talons exercising firm hold the
Poise regal, majestic.
It's time for coronation.

ACTIVITY SOMEWHAT

The street led to shops
Shopkeepers and their wares
Carts no way behind
Selling fruits, snacks
Hot, spicy, orange red
Farm produce hanging
Dangling, far and wide
To the swaying breeze
Warm, rising air
Now dust laden
As are the clothes
Pegged atop the roof on the line
No more wet
Twin temples dotting the
Far end, silent somewhat in the
Pervading noon past
Visitors none at this hour.

BEING GRANNY

Oval spectacles string bound
To face fitted rotund round
Brown, wrinkled, aged sound
Slow, gradual moves around
In a house clay fed
Brown, wet red
Roofed plant matter, dried, dead
No further to animate objects wed
In easy chair recline
While the rest sup and dine
Homemade wine
Or supple betel vine
Knits wool to woolen ordained
Texture fine or coarse grained
Mind, energy, passion drained
To good avail her heyday trained
Grey white hair
Expertise deft and flair
Ripe, mature, cozy care
Contentment writ large, utmost fair.

WAKING UP FOR A CAUSE

The stretch wakes up every morning to
Coconut palm, mango
Jackfruit and more likewise
Some fruit laden
Rest green immature yet to
Scent laden air profuse
Sweet, intoxicating the
Wayfarer few the
Objects animate the
Moss, herb, shrub
Creeper and vine floral ornate
Trees big fat wide or
Others of the kin
Crows and raven
Cacophony new
Two pied cuckoos and an
Oriental magpie robin in
Sharp, contrast deep
Mellifluous, magical
Lullaby-like to
Lull us to sleep
Again to rise the next day.

THE ROOM IN THE LODGE

Two men, two stations
Two beds in actuality
In a lodge, setting out in the
Morning to return the
Same evening, today
Tomorrow, all days
Except the Sundays
Earmarked on purpose to
Gossip, sip tea or
Smoke a cigarette or two
Yellow, stained packets
Like the walls on the exterior to
Rain and tropics exposed
Wooden blinds maneuvered up and down
Lets in air humid and
Sunlight colorless, white in the
Room to us assigned
Close to the city square the
Passing trams, their bells
Ringing and the temple gong close by
Further intensified.

Inside the ornate table and a
Couple of rickety chairs with
Age weakened, feeble a
Blown fuse aggravating the woes
Darkness, sweat desperate
Light far beyond.

A CUTLER HE REMAINS

The knife sharpener owned a shop
Old and spacious enough to
House scissors, knives to be
Sharpened or yet still a
Cutler he was
Operating the grinding wheel
Big, round, circular
Emanating noise loud and
Fireworks, sparks yellow and bright
Seen against the walls dark
Day and night
Dense beard white
Bespectacled, bicycle astride
On his way to work and
Home in the night a
Cutler he still is
Mellower, ripe with
Age sharpened.

THE STEAM LOCOMOTIVE

The big black steam locomotive
Gathers steam
In no time will it
Chug along
Belching grey smoke
Upwards into the sky the
Wheels having initialized
Engine set in motion the
Station a far cry in some while the
Giant is on the move
Past human settlements
Stage carriages, farms the
Stellar design at the front
Grand light adorning its head to
Brighten its way
Whistling to glory
All awhile.

ON DHARAVI

One room abodes line the
Lanes dark narrow
Inhabited by the teeming men the
Metropolis and its populace
Out to eke a living
In the shops on the periphery
Double storied some
Selling furniture, fabric
Leather, hide and more added
While the alleys see women queuing up to
Get the water necessary
For the daily chores
Adolescents frequent the
Intersections engaged in
Meaningful business to
Earn a livelihood to
Rise above the hardships to
Mitigate the suffering for
Betterment, freedom and
Living anew.

BLACK CRICKETS

The area abounds in crickets
Big, black, zigzag
Startling you with sudden flight an
Airy leap
Short, though
Stridulating their legs or wings at
Will to produce a
Sound shrill, quite loud as
Would resonate in the
Darkness empty, profound to be
Silenced only by
Advancing footsteps to be
Tread with care
Lest we inhibit the
Proliferation, the thrive in
Full earnest, ease.

WATCHING CROWS

Morning wakes you up
Crows calling out atop the
Fig tree just behind
Scores of them
Communicating amongst themselves or
Other species
Day having begun
Sleep well past
Black, gray
Grayish black into the
Hour bright
Sun having risen
Men and womenfolk
Their activities commenced
Daily chores, over and over again
As do the crows and the brethren
Now croaking, next a
Quick flap of the wings
One, two and all of them
The murder proceeds
Like they say
As the crow flies.

NOT TO BE COWED DOWN

On being gainfully employed on
Getting to know the
Chance meeting
Conversations of duration short on
Developing affinity and
Inhaling the realm
Around deep on
Being exalted and
Being revered on
Vision getting impaired and
Eyes closed offering
Sight more intense on
Oneself being spun the
Head reeling the
World rotating the
Planet Earth revolving the more
Churning out the crux of the Matter
Joy, Pleasure, Ecstasy.

RAIN AND FURY

No more light
The breeze fortified
Dust blew
Pigeons flew
Way below
The wind playing spoilsport
Off the playing arena, the court
Clouds thickened
Hold weakened
The drizzle commenced
In no time a downpour
One deafening roar
A flash emerged
Roads submerged
The thunder, the bolt
Cloudy revolt
Big fat drops
Scurrying cops
Power snapped, the hardship, the toil
Misery, agony and turmoil.

www.ingramcontent.com/pod-product-compliance
Lightning Source LLC
LaVergne TN
LVHW041212150826
845673LV00001B/368